D1091651

BEING a GOOD GUEST

The Child's World

Published by The Child's World®
1980 Lookout Drive • Mankato, MN 56003-1705
800-599-READ • www.childsworld.com

Acknowledgments
The Child's World®: Mary Berendes, Publishing Director
The Design Lab: Design and production
Red Line Editorial: Editorial direction

ISBN 9781614732242
LCCN 2012932439

Printed in the United States of America
Mankato, MN
July 2012
PA02126

ABOUT THE AUTHOR

Ann Ingalls writes stories and poems for people of all ages as well as resource materials for parents and teachers. She was a teacher for many years and enjoys working with children. When she isn't writing, she enjoys spending time with her family and friends, traveling, reading, knitting, and playing with her cats.

ABOUT THE ILLUSTRATOR

Ronnie Rooney took art classes constantly as a child. She was always drawing and painting at her mom's kitchen table. She got her BFA in painting from the University of Massachusetts at Amherst and her MFA in Illustration from Savannah College of Art and Design in Savannah, Georgia. She now lives and works in Fort Lewis, Washington. Her plan is to pass her love of art and sports on to her two young children.

CONTENTS

Good Guest Manners

You have been **invited** to a party! What is the first thing you do? Look at the day and time on the **invitation**. Check your calendar. If you can go, reply to the invitation. Let your friend know that you will be there.

You are going to be a guest. Guests go to parties or just visit at someone's house. That sounds fun! Are you going to be a good guest? If you have manners you will. Manners let your host know that you feel great about being a guest.

Party Help

If you are going to a party, ask if you can bring something. Maybe your friend needs a ball for a game. Maybe you can bring a pizza to pass around.

Be on time. Do not spoil the party by holding everyone else up.

If you can, ask if you can arrive a little early. You can help set up for the event. Fan the napkins on the table. Put out the funny party hats. Make tiny sandwiches or a giant hoagie. Your host will **appreciate** your help.

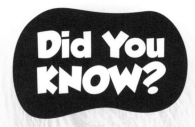

Did You KNOW?

Bring a small gift to thank your host. Flowers or chocolates make great host gifts.

Hats and Shoes

Take off your hat when you enter someone's house. Do it even if your hair is really wild. And make sure to take off your shoes. Leave them by the door on a mat. This is really important on snowy and rainy days. No one wants sloppy, slushy, or muddy floors.

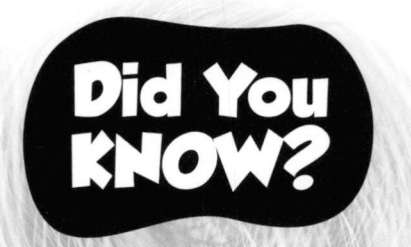

Did You KNOW?

In Japan people take off their shoes just inside the front door. They put on slippers left by the host at the door.

No Surprises

Call before you drop in on a friend or **relative**. Do not show up on someone's doorstep with your suitcase. Your friend may have other plans.

If you are invited, be sure to let your friend know when you will be there. Also say when you will be going home. Do not stay as long as you please.

No Snooping!

Stay with your friend at his home. Do not wander off on your own.

If you go to the bathroom, do not open closets or drawers. It is not nice to be nosey.

Is it a sleepover? And did you forget to bring your toothpaste? Ask your host if you can use some of hers.

Rules and Respect

Respect the rules of the house. Your friend's family may have different rules than your family. Ask your host if you do not know the family's rules.

Pick up after yourself. Put toys away after you play with them. Leave the bathroom as clean as a whistle.

If you break something, offer to fix it or buy a new one. Tell your host how sorry you are, too.

And if you are sleeping over, keep quiet late at night. Whisper and walk quietly. Do not stomp around like a dinosaur. You do not want to wake anyone up.

Eating a Meal

If you are lucky, you may be asked to stay for a meal. Always wait for the host to offer. Never help yourself to food from the kitchen.

When the meal is over, tell your host how great the meal tasted. Ask if you can help clear the table. Bring your plate to the kitchen. Offer to help clean the dishes, too. It is a great way to say, "Thank you" for a meal.

Did You KNOW?

In Turkey, asking for more food is great. It is a compliment to the host.

Be Friendly

Talk with your friend's family. Be **polite** and answer questions. Remember to say, "Please," "Thank you," and "Excuse me."

Be friendly, but do not be in the way. Everyone needs a bit of space. If your host is yawning, it might be time to go home. It is not time to tell him about every comic book in your **collection**.

A Bit More Polite

When it is time to leave, thank your host. Send a thank you note when you get home. Tell the host how much fun you had.

Return the favor, too. Invite your friends to your house sometime. This time you can be the host. Good guests also make great hosts!

Quick QUIZ

Put your new guest manners in action with this pop quiz! Will you choose the right rules?

When you get an invitation to a party, you should:
a. toss it on the floor.
b. not reply and then show up at the party.
c. call the host to tell her if you can come.
d. not read it.

It is fine to show up at your friend's house with a suitcase:
a. on your birthday.
b. when you have already made plans.
c. when you want to spend the night.
d. when your friend's parents are not home.

If you forget your toothpaste you can:
a. look in all of the drawers in the bathroom.
b. look in all of the closets for toothpaste.
c. ask your friend if you can use some of his toothpaste.
d. use your friend's toothpaste without asking.

When you come into a host's house, you should:

a. take off your coat, hat, and boots and put them out of the way.
b. make mud tracks in the kitchen.
c. throw your coat right in front of the door.
d. leave your coat, hat, and boots on and sit on the couch.

After you have eaten at your friend's house you should:

a. offer to clear the dishes.
b. offer to help wash the dishes.
c. say, "Thank you for the meal."
d. all of the above.

Please do not write in the book!

Glossary

appreciate (uh-PREE-shee-ate): To appreciate is to enjoy or value someone or something. He will appreciate Jon's help later.

collection (kuh-LEK-shuhn): A collection is a group of things a person gathers over a long time. Mary has a cool comic book collection.

compliment (KOM-pluh-ment): To compliment is to show that you think another person has done something well. That is a nice compliment to her cooking.

invitation (in-vit-TAY-shuhn): An invitation is when someone asks you to do something. Tracy got her invitation in the mail.

invited (in-VITE-id): To be invited is to be asked to do something or go somewhere. Max is invited to Brady's party.

polite (puh-LITE): To be polite is to have good manners. It is polite to answer questions.

relative (REL-uh-tiv): A relative is a member of your family. Did a relative or friend invite you?

respect (ri-SPEKT): To have respect is to care for another person's feelings or treat his or her home with care. Show respect by taking off your shoes.

Web Sites

Visit our Web site for links about guest manners:
childsworld.com/links

Note to Parents, Teachers, and Librarians: We routinely verify our Web links to make sure they are safe and active sites. So encourage your readers to check them out!

Books

Burstein, John. *Manners, Please!: Why It Pays to be Polite.* New York: Crabtree, 2011.

Eberly, Sheryl. *365 Manners Kids Should Know: Games, Activities, and Other Fun Ways to Help Children Learn Etiquette.* New York: Three Rivers Press, 2001.

Espeland, Pamela. *Dude, That's Rude!* Minneapolis, MN: Free Spirit Publishing, 2007.

Index